Children's Bulletin Clip-Art Book

Virginia Lettinga

BakerBooks

A Division of Baker Book House Co
Grand Rapids, Michigan 49516

W9-DES-392

Contents

Guidelines

Generic Children's Bulletin Headings

Old Testament Stories

New Testament Stories—Life of Christ

Advent

Christmas

Ministry Years

Palm Sunday

Easter

Ascension

Miscellaneous

Baptism

The Lord's Supper

Prayer

Pauline Epistles

Seasonal

For me, the vision to create children's bulletins was born out of two frustrations: the frustration of sitting in a church pew behind tuned-out, squirmy children, and frustration with the church elder who thought the solution was, "They just have to learn to sit still."

Church is not to teach children to "sit still." The Sunday morning church service gathers the body of Christ together to learn and to worship the Lord; if we take seriously Jesus' words to "let the little ones come to me, and do not forbid them . . . ," then we must also include children in the teaching and worship of the regular worship service. Children's bulletins are a good way to include children in a part of the worship service and can counter some of the messages we often unwittingly teach our children about church: sermons and prayers are for tuning out and for others (adults). Patterns set down during early childhood are difficult to unlearn. Tuned-out children often become sleeping adults.

Goals to Keep in Mind

The primary purpose of children's bulletins, to me, is to help children participate in the *teaching* portion of the worship service. To achieve this I work toward several smaller goals. Children's bulletins should:

encourage the children to think about the Bible passage

reinforce the sermon's main point from a child's perspective

relate the sermon or text to something concrete with which the children can identify

encourage appropriate behavior (second graders and older should be encouraged to listen to the sermon, for example.)

I try to avoid jokes and games, however clever, that might distract from the service; the danger of creating yet another acceptable way to tune out is very real.

Start by Assessing Your Situation:

What your children's bulletin should look like depends on *whom you expect to use it*. I have designed children's bulletins for three major age groups:

preschool

young school (kindergarten-second grade)

mid-school (third-sixth grade)

Many churches print up entirely separate bulletins for the different age groups. I've had success with printing "Tough Stuff" questions for older children in the margins of the simple mazes and dot-to-dots designed for the younger children.

What your children's bulletin should look like also depends on *when you expect the children to use it*. Should the children fill out all the mazes and crossword puzzles as soon as they sit down in the pew? Do you want them to pull out the bulletin and fill it out during the sermon? I regularly place a notice in the adult bulletin asking parents to help their children join in singing and prayers early in the service, and save the children's bulletin till the sermon. I also try to include games and questions which depend on the sermon itself.

Information You Need to Know for Each Bulletin

I usually call the church on Wednesday for answers to these questions:

1. What is next Sundays' sermon's title?
2. What is the sermon's text?
3. What is the sermon's outline?
4. Are there any special events at church this Sunday? (a missionary's report, baptism, etc.)
5. What is the day's offering for?

Equipment and Format

A good computer graphics program makes producing children's bulletins easy, but I usually prepare it on my dining-room table with the following tools:

A good pair of scissors. (I cut and glue everything together.)

Rubber cement (other glues work, but may pucker up the paper if you're not careful.)

White paper. I usually use standard 8 1/2" x 11" typing paper, but semi-translucent marker paper is easier to work with (your pens are less likely to smear and you can trace things more easily.)

Good black pens of various widths.

White-Out.

Graph paper to use as a guide to line up things.

Photocopies of the pictures, puzzles, and other ideas and images from this book, which you intend to use and adapt.

Tailor your children's bulletin to the copying equipment it will be produced on. Most copying machines need at least a 1/2" outside margin—some need a larger margin. No copying machine functions well with large blocks of solid black. Photocopying will hide most lines from your cut-and-glue job. If you need to, touch up your "master copy" with White Out.

Evaluate your children's bulletins

To do a good job with children's bulletins, it's important to know what worked and didn't work for the children in your congregation. Are the mazes too easy? Too frustrating? Could people figure out your instructions? I occasionally ask the Sunday school teachers to walk in with a few children's bulletins and ask the children what they liked best and least on them. Sometimes I ask the older children to fill out and turn in a bulletin for a reward.

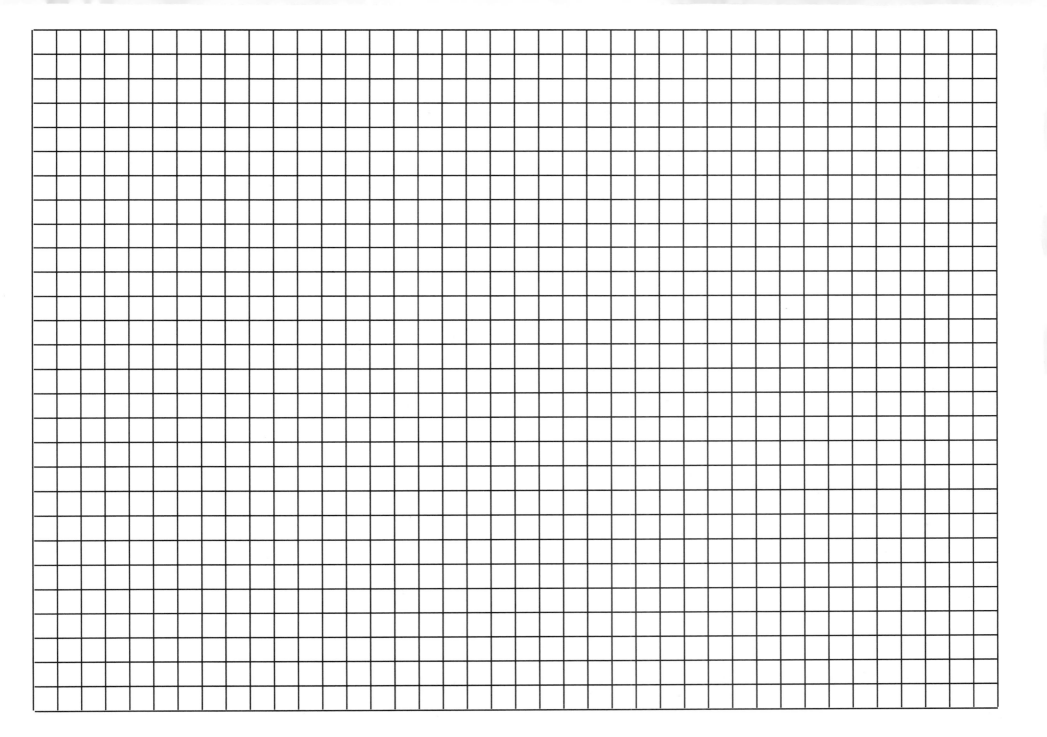

CHILDREN'S BULLETIN

CHILDREN'S BULLETIN

CHILDREN'S BULLETIN

Children's Bulletin

CHILDREN'S BULLETIN

CHILDREN'S BULLETIN

CHILDREN'S BULLETIN

CHILDREN'S BULLETIN

CHILDREN'S BULLETIN

CHILDREN'S BULLETIN

CHILDREN'S BULLETIN

CHILDREN'S BULLETIN

CHILDREN'S BULLETIN

CHILDREN'S BULLETIN

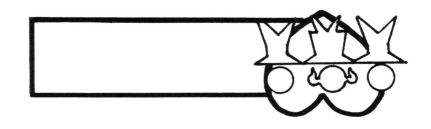

Old Testament Stories

_M_Z_NG GR_C_

Fill in the missing vowels to read the title of this song. What is your favorite verse of this song?

The Song's Story

It was written by John Newton about the time of the American Revolution. John Newton was the captain of a ship that carried Africans to America to be slaves. When John became a Christian he was amazed that Jesus was willing to love someone who had done such awful things to these Africans.

Can you find two crosses that are exactly the same?
Can you guess what each picture in the crosses means?

Genesis 3 Adam and Eve broke God's rule and now they are hiding from God.
• Can you find Adam and Eve?
• How many animals can you find?

Carefully fill in all the squares with dots.

Our lives should also be a
JOURNEY OF

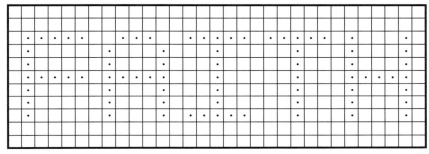

Fill in the blanks with the right letters to find out about our faith journey.

[ ] ix our eyes on Jesus . . .
Hebrews 12:2

Love [ ] lways protects, always trusts, always hopes, always perseveres.
1 Corinthians 13:7

[ ] t does not envy, it does not boast.
1 Corinthians 13:4

[ ] rust in the Lord with all your heart.
Proverbs 3:5

[ ] old to the good. Avoid every kind of evil.
1 Thessalonians 5:21, 22

Genesis 12:1–8

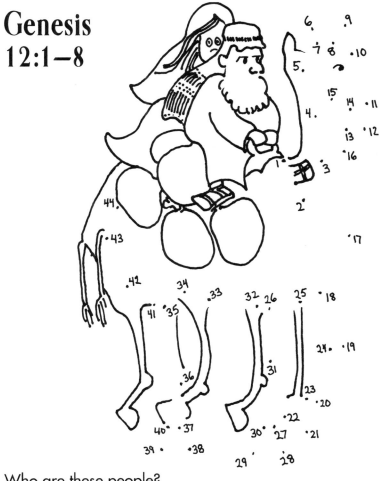

Who are these people?
Where are they going?
Why are they going?

Abraham and Sarah took a JOURNEY OF FAITH; they left their old home to go to a land God promised them.

THE PROMISED LAND

Tough Question: "Abraham" and "Sarah" are names God gave to Abram and Sarai. Can you find the chapter in Genesis where the new names are given?

WORD MAZE

Trace the path of the words in the Bible verse through the maze of letters. What shape do you see?

"ABRAHAM OBEYED AND WENT EVEN THOUGH HE DID NOT KNOW WHERE HE WAS GOING."

(Hebrews 11:8)

```
F  P  L  G  T  A  T  M  N  O  L  J  P  V
L  O  V  E  X  B  L  F  G  B  C  E  N  P
S  B  A  T  L  R  Q  S  N  V  Z  S  T  Q
N  S  D  F  V  A  R  M  I  L  C  U  B  B
M  O  P  T  C  H  T  U  O  V  W  S  B  L
G  D  H  J  L  A  C  C  G  D  F  G  N  Z
F  V  X  S  P  M  Z  D  S  W  X  L  F  T
D  E  Y  E  B  O  T  T  A  W  E  H  E  R
A  L  L  B  X  V  C  B  F  L  T  V  X  E
N  W  M  L  R  R  L  V  W  X  Z  H  S  H
D  W  E  N  T  E  B  B  T  K  N  O  W  W
S  T  B  L  V  V  R  N  O  F  B  P  T  U
Y  Z  B  C  D  E  K  T  N  G  E  K  U  L
T  S  O  M  E  N  L  M  D  Z  P  L  S  R
R  M  A  N  P  T  F  A  I  T  H  Z  O  F
C  D  Z  H  B  H  Q  O  D  X  K  L  N  M
L  O  B  V  L  O  R  D  E  T  N  U  V  Z
S  G  R  X  C  U  G  H  H  V  B  L  R  S
```

How did Joseph's brothers feel when they were taken to his house? (See Genesis 43:18.)

Draw in their faces.

How many circles, triangles, squares, and rectangles can you find?

What did Joseph's steward say to them?

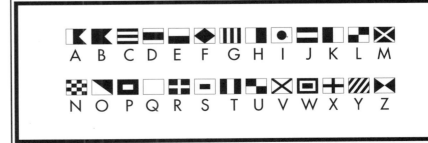

Show Joseph's brothers the way from Canaan to Egypt.

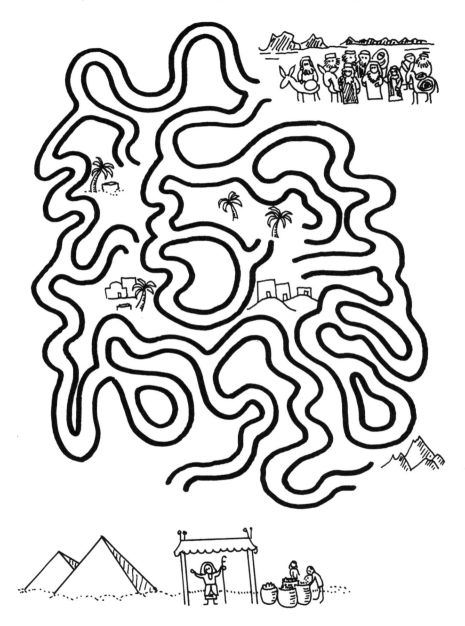

What great trouble did God use to bring Joseph and his family together in Egypt?

Fill in the boxes with the correct words. The first letters spell out the answer.

What did Jacob send his sons to buy? (Genesis 43:2)
☐ ☐ ☐ ☐

Jacob told his sons to take along a gift—some pistachio nuts and what other nut? (Genesis 43:11)
☐ ☐ ☐ ☐ ☐ ☐ ☐

What does Jacob pray that God will grant his sons? (Genesis 43:14)
☐ ☐ ☐ ☐ ☐ ☐

Another name for Jacob. (Genesis 43:8)
☐ ☐ ☐ ☐ ☐ ☐ ☐

What time of day did the brothers eat with Joseph? (Genesis 43:16)
☐ ☐ ☐ ☐

What country still had food when everyone else was hungry? (Genesis 42:1)
☐ ☐ ☐ ☐ ☐

What kind of faces do people have when they're hungry?

Genesis 44 Crossword Puzzle

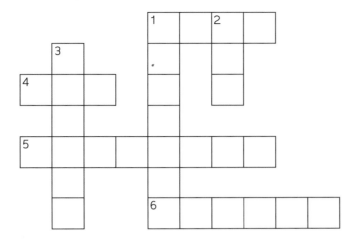

Down
1. He chased after the brothers.
2. This was found in Benjamin's sack.
3. The ruler of all Egypt after Pharaoh.

Across
1. The brothers carried the food in this.
4. Who did the brothers say uncovered their guilt?
5. The youngest of the twelve brothers.
6. The brothers rode on this animal.

What do you think Joseph's special silver cup might have looked like?
Draw a picture of it here.

CHILDREN'S BULLETIN

Who is this? Whose sack is he looking in? Why?
(See Genesis 44:1–2.)

Help Joseph's steward find the brothers who've started for Canaan.

START

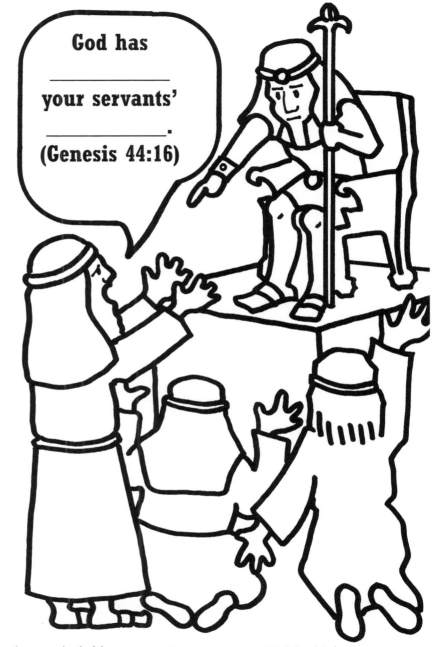

What guilt did he mean? (See Genesis 37:23–28.)

WHAT IS WRONG WITH THIS PICTURE?

Can you find the ten "modern" things that don't belong with Joseph and his brothers?

CHILDREN'S BULLETIN

Who is in trouble? Why? (See Genesis 44:12.)

Many years earlier, it had been Judah's idea to sell his brother Joseph as a slave. What does he say when it looks like his youngest brother Benjamin might become a slave?

See Genesis 44 for the rest of the story.

Can you unscramble these letters to find the twelve brothers' names?

NIJAEMBN

ADG

HOSJPO

LIEV

RISASHCA

ADN

RAHSE

DAUJH

NEBURE

OMISNE

ULNUBZE

PAATNILH

If you're stuck, see Genesis 35:23–26

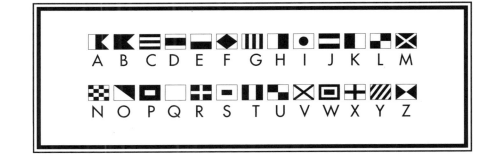

CAN YOU FIND THE NAMES OF JACOB'S TWELVE SONS?

See Genesis 35:23–26 for a list of their names.

```
X  L  R  F  P  I  N  S
G  M  X  T  V  J  A  R
A  S  H  E  R  O  P  Q
D  Z  L  R  P  S  H  T
P  E  X  B  M  E  T  R
J  B  V  E  L  P  A  R
G  U  R  N  T  H  L  E
S  L  D  J  C  X  I  U
H  U  X  A  F  G  H  B
L  N  S  M  H  K  W  E
P  S  S  I  M  E  O  N
I  D  A  N  S  X  H  F
```

Joseph has prepared a special dinner. Who is it for? (See Genesis 43:16.)

The plates and bowls are empty. Draw in the food for the feast.

Can you find the one picture that is **different** in each row?

Whose food sack was the different one? See Genesis 44:1–12.

Who watched sheep in Jacob's family? See Genesis 37:2.

Who dreamed about the sun, moon, and stars? What was the dream about? See Genesis 37:9–11.

What did Joseph's brothers look up and see after they had put him in the dry well? See Genesis 37:25.

CHILDREN'S BULLETIN

Who is the lonely old man in the tent?
Why is he worried?
Why is he sad?
See Genesis 43:1–14.

ONE MAN TWO NAMES

GENESIS 45:26–28

When Joseph's father learns that Joseph is still alive and can't believe the news, the Bible calls him

CAJBO. __ __ __ __ __

(Unscramble the letters and write the name above.)

When Joseph's father believes the good news the Bible calls him

RILESA. __ __ __ __ __ __

(Unscramble the letters and write the name above.)

Can you draw a five-pointed star in this circle so that each point touches one letter of Jacob's name?

K V J E D
B A
R P
N S
O C
L U T

Jacob found it hard to believe the news that Joseph was alive until he saw what Joseph had sent to him.

Connect the dots so that you too can see what Joseph sent.

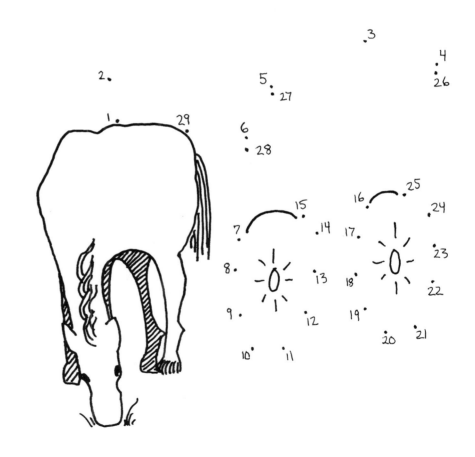

Old Jacob and all his children, grandchildren, servants, and animals moved down to Egypt. Help them find the way.

CHILDREN'S BULLETIN

Carefully fill in the dotted squares to learn the news that shocked Joseph's brothers.

Draw in the Faces

Joseph wept for joy.

How did his brothers feel at first?

(See Genesis 45:3.)

How did his old father feel when he learned Joseph was alive?

GENESIS 45:1-9
FILL IN THE BLANKS

1. _____ heard Joseph weeping.

2. Joseph asked, "Is my _____ still _____?"

3. Joseph's brothers couldn't answer because they were so _____.

4. God sent Joseph to Egypt in order to save _____.

5. There have been _____ years of famine and _____ years are left.

6. _____, not his brothers, really sent Joseph to Egypt.

God's Providence is the name for the kind of caring and planning we see God doing for Joseph and his family. God also cares for us this way!

When hard-hearted Pharaoh kept refusing to let the Israelites go, God finally sent one last plague . . .

No!

The Angel of Death

But to keep the Israelites safe from the Angel of Death, each family had to find a spotless lamb and kill it.

The meat they fixed for a special meal. The blood of the lamb they used to mark each Israelite home. When the Angel of Death saw the blood it did not visit those homes.

How did the Egyptians look when they discovered the Angel of Death had killed all their firstborn children?

How did the Israelites look when Pharaoh finally let them go?

Where did God tell Moses and the Israelites that they should put the lamb's blood? Can you draw it in? (See Exodus 12:21–23.)

God told the Israelites to choose a perfect lamb each year.

This lamb was killed as a sacrifice to God. A sacrifice showed God they were sorry they had done wrong.

Jesus was sacrificed for us when he died on the cross. Because of this, he is called . . .

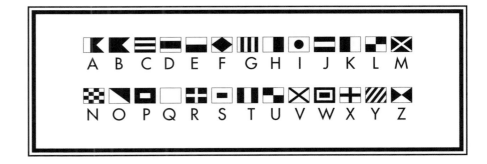

A	B	C	D	E	F	G	H	I	J	K	L	M
N	O	P	Q	R	S	T	U	V	W	X	Y	Z

Can you uncode the secret message?

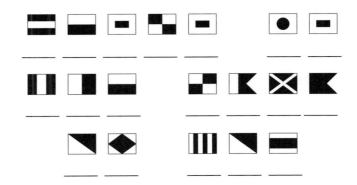

Abraham and his son Isaac went to Mount Moriah to pray and sacrifice to God. First find the way to Mount Moriah, then find the sacrifice God provided.

Samson's body was very strong, but he was not a strong leader for God. Read Judges 14–16. What do you think his biggest mistake was? Draw a picture here.

After church, ask your parents what they thought Samson's biggest mistake was.

GOD'S STRONG MAN?

Fill in the dotted squares.

What Was Samson's Riddle?

Look up Judges 14:14 and fill in the blanks.

— — —   — —   — — —

— — — — — ,

— — — — — — — — — — — — — —

— — — ;   — — — — —

— — —   — — — — — — ,

— — — — — — — — — —

— — — — — .

Where in Judges 14 is the answer given?_____

How many bees can you find on these two pages? Why are they here? (The exact number of bees is on page one under the name "Samson.")

Bible People Riddles

Can you figure out who these riddles are talking about?

Her baby boy
has brought us joy.
He paid our sin
now we're forgiv'n.

The king of beasts didn't claw or bite
this man who prayed to our God of light.

He plucked a string
and became a king.

In his fall
we've sinned all.

He went afloat
in a boat
with bear and goat
and fox and stoat.

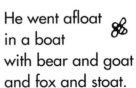

This "Rock" who
walked upon the waves,
cried out to Jesus
to be saved.

Judges 6 Crossword Puzzle

Down

1. Gideon placed this on the threshing floor for a sign (v. 37).
4. Who visited Gideon while he was threshing wheat (v. 12)?
5. Gideon comes from this tribe (v. 15).
6. Gideon destroyed Baal's altar at this time (v. 27).
8. Once the fleece was wet with this, once it was dry (vv. 37–40).
10. The bull Gideon was to sacrifice was _____ years old (v. 25).

Across

2. Gideon built an _____ to God after the angel left (v. 24).
3. What idol's altar did Gideon tear down (v. 25)?
7. The angel called him a "mighty warrior" but he had many doubts.
9. What did the Israelites do to deserve their troubles (v. 1)?
11. Whose wooden pole did he burn (v. 26)?

CHILDREN'S BULLETIN

Who is attacking the Israelites?

Why did God let this happen?

Where are the Israelites?

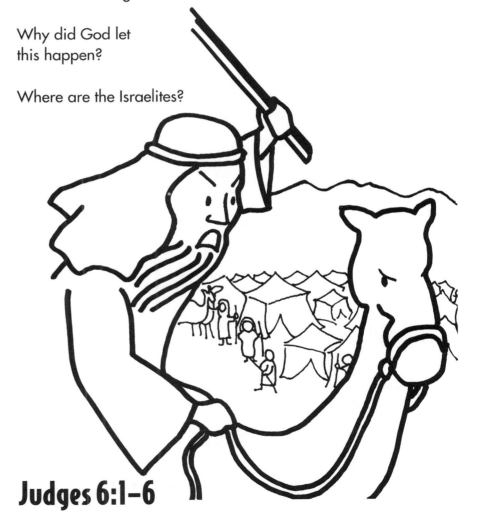

Judges 6:1–6

God heard the Israelites cry for help.

The _ _ _ _ is
with _ _ _ ,
_ _ _ _ _ _
_ _ _ _ _ _ _ _ . Judges 6:12

BUT...

Gideon is full of
DOUBTS

In Judges 6 God shows him three signs to give him confidence.

Draw a picture of the things used in the first sign (Judges 6:20–21).

Draw a picture of the things used in the second and third signs (Judges 6:36–40).

Even though Gideon had many doubts we usually remember him as a great warrior of the Lord and a man of faith. Read Judges 7 later today to find out why.

What was the Bible text for today?

Draw a picture of it to remind your parents of what you heard in church today.

CHILDREN'S BULLETIN

Two sad women.

Where have they come from?

Where are they going?

Unscramble the letters on the signs to see.

Naomi left Bethlehem with two sons and her husband. Years later she returned a penniless widow. Can you find her path between Bethlehem and Moab?

Ruth 1:16

What did Ruth say to Naomi that made such a difference? Fill in the words.

BOAZ WAS NAOMI'S KINSMAN

A "kinsman" is a relative. Draw pictures of some of your kinsmen and women below.

SERMON SQUARES

Listen carefully. Cross out the words you hear the pastor say in the sermon today.

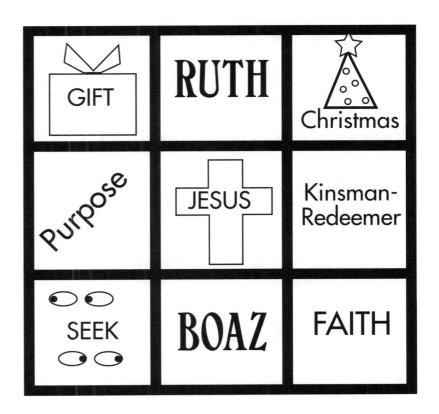

Three in a row? Good. All nine? Superstar!

Ruth GLEANED behind Boaz's REAPERS.

The reapers grasped the grain  in one hand and cut it with a sickle in the other hand. They tied the grain into big bundles (sheaves). Poor people, like Ruth, could follow behind the reapers and pick up the stalks of grain they accidently dropped. Boaz told his reapers to help Ruth, though. What did he tell them to do?

Ruth 2:12

What did Boaz say to Ruth?

A B C D E F G H I J K L M N O P Q R S T U V W X Y Z

Add the vertical lines (lines that go up and down) to the letters below so that you can read the Bible verse. See Psalm 37:4 for help. EXAMPLE: ⊨ is E and ∟ is L.

DELIGHT YOURSELF
IN THE LORD AND
HE WILL GIVE
YOU THE DESIRES
OF YOUR HEART.

Connect the dots.

What does the "desire of your heart" mean?

1. Listen to the pastor as he explains it.
2. Ask your parents after church.

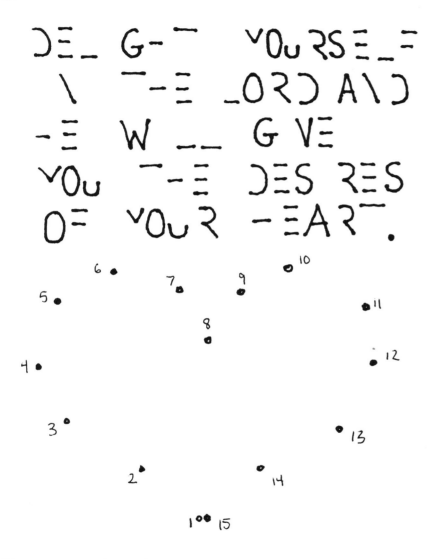

1. How many trumpets can you find on this page?
2. How many trumpets are played in church today?
3. Color the letters. What do they say?

HARDER STUFF: Can you find any psalms where we are told to praise the Lord with the sound of trumpets?

CHILDREN'S BULLETIN

PRAISE THE LORD, YOU HIS ANGELS, YOU MIGHTY ONES WHO DO HIS BIDDING, WHO OBEY HIS WORD.
PSALM 103:20

Jesus taught us to pray, ". . . your will be done on earth as it is in heaven . . ."

Let us go to the house of the Lord!

Psalm 122:1

Help the children get to church.

CHILDREN'S BULLETIN

Fill in the spaces that have dots in them.

WE SING   WE PRAY   WE LISTEN   WE SHARE

Psalms 42 and 43

are about hoping in God even when you are unhappy or sad.

Draw sad faces here.

Draw hopeful faces here.

HARDER STUFF: Write down every word you know that shows unhappiness (for example, "sad," "miserable,"). How many words do you know? Check Psalms 42 and 43 for other words.

CHILDREN'S BULLETIN

Sometimes it is hard to have hope. Fill in the missing letters in this sad song. See Psalm 137 for help.

Can you find the two matching items in each row?

Did you recognize the two rows with people praying? The psalm-singer who wrote Psalm 145 probably raised his hands and eyes to God like the last row.

I will exalt you, my God the King!

Psalm 145:1

What does "exalt" mean? The psalm-singer used another word that means the same thing in the next sentence. It is

___ ___ ___ ___ ___ ___

If we don't act out of love during the rest of the week, God is not pleased with our singing or praying or listening to the sermon.

WHAT CAN YOU DO?

In each heart below, draw a picture of what you can do for others this week.

OLD TESTAMENT PROPHETS

Spoke to God's people before Jesus was born. They told people how to live for God.

Jeremiah   **Amos**   **Isaiah**   **Jonah**   **Ezekiel**

1. Circle the prophet the pastor is talking about.
2. Fit all their names into the puzzle below.

LISTEN TO THE PASTOR: (fill in the blanks)

In what can we place _____

when _____ seems to have forgotten us?

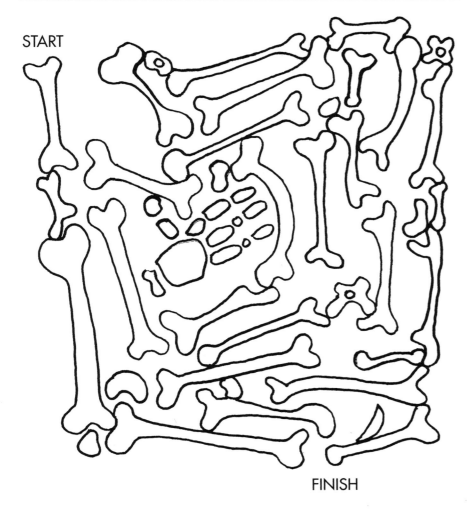

START

FINISH

God led Ezekiel to a valley full of old, dry bones. God's Spirit could make even those bones live! God's Spirit will make his people live too!

Read Ezekiel 37:1–14 (or listen to the preacher read the Bible). Draw a picture of what you think it looked like when the Spirit brought the bones to life.

Jesus is the king of prophecy. Hundreds of years before Jesus was born in Bethlehem, the prophet Isaiah spoke about him. He explained what sort of king Jesus would be.

Draw the people who have been healed. What do their faces look like?

Fill in the letters under the code to read what Isaiah said about Jesus.

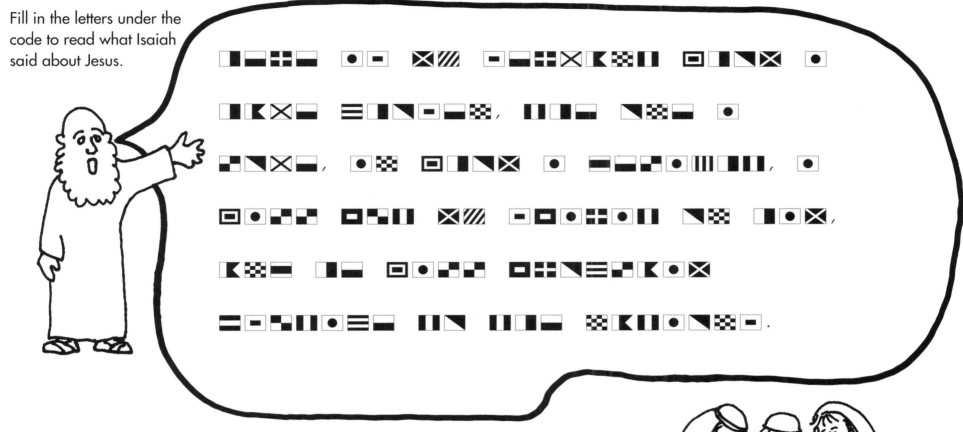

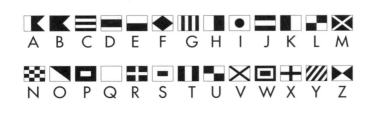

New Testament Stories—Life of Christ

Advent
Christmas
Ministry Years
Palm Sunday
Easter
Ascension

PROPHETS

Many years before Jesus' birth, the Old Testament prophets told the people what the Messiah would be like and called them to faithfulness.

Place the following names in the crossword:

ISAIAH
JEREMIAH
AMOS
OBADIAH
JONAH

THE GLORY OF THE LORD RISES UPON YOU —ISAIAH 60:1

Advent is four special weeks of waiting before Christmas. It helps us remember how the Old Testament believers waited. Draw a flame on the first candle. (Can you find the four letters for this candle's name?)

BETHLEHEM

The City  the King!

David, Ruth's great-grandson, was born here. So was a much greater king. What was his name?

Help Mary and Joseph find Bethlehem's inn.

Today begins the second week in Advent. Draw flames on two of the candles. Can you find the hidden letters for the candle's name?

This shepherd wasn't watching his sheep carefully. How many lost sheep can you find?

The third candle in our Advent wreath is called the "Shepherd Candle." Draw flames on three of the candles.

HARDER STUFF: How many words can you make out of the letters in the word SHEPHERD?

_____

_____

I BRING YOU GOOD NEWS OF GREAT JOY!

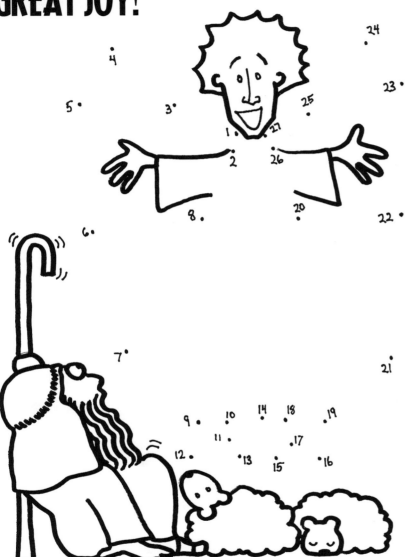

Connect the dots and color the picture.

Today is the fourth Sunday of Advent. Draw a flame on four candles today. The fourth candle is called the "Angel Candle." Can you find the words of the angel's message (Luke 2) hidden among the Christmas greens?

WHAT DOES THE BIBLE REALLY SAY?

○ TRUE ○ FALSE 1. The wise men saw Jesus in the manger.

○ TRUE ○ FALSE 2. The Christmas angels had wings.

○ TRUE ○ FALSE 3. There were some animals in the stable.

○ TRUE ○ FALSE 4. Three wise men visited Jesus.

○ TRUE ○ FALSE 5. Baby Jesus never cried.

1. FALSE. Mary and Joseph had moved into a house by the time the wise men visited them (Matthew 2:11).
2. PROBABLY FALSE. The only angels the Bible describes as having wings (Isaiah 6:2) have six wings, not two.
3. PROBABLY TRUE. But the Bible does not tell us. Jesus was born in a stable, though, not a barn. There were probably camels and donkeys, not cows and sheep, there.
4. FALSE. The Bible tells us that there were three gifts, not that there were three wise men. Maybe there were three. Maybe two. Maybe ten.
5. FALSE. The Bible teaches us that Jesus was fully human. All human babies cry sometime.

Draw flames on the Advent candles. Can you read the candles' names? Color in the dotted shapes to find the name of the middle candle.

The people walking in darkness have seen a great light;
on those living in the land of darkness a light has dawned.
For to us a child is born! (Isaiah 9:2, 6)

Draw a cross in the center of the light.

Draw the flame on the first candle. Color the holly berries.

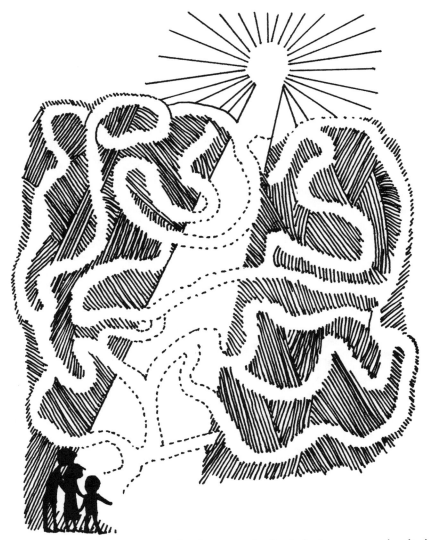

Help the people find their way to the light.

ADVENT
helps us
remember
Jesus's
coming

Jesus **CAME** as a in

Jesus **COMES** in our ♡ s.

Jesus will **COME BACK** again!

Who is "THE WORD"?

To find out, cross out each B, M, F, L, O, and W.

B	J	M	E	F	S	L	U	F	S	O
C	M	H	W	R	O	I	L	S	T	M
B	M	B	F	O	B	M	W	O	L	F

The Bible uses many different names for Jesus to help us under-stand different things about him. List as many different names for Jesus as you can find in the prophet Isaiah's chapters 7, 9, and 11. At home later, ask your parents to tell you as many of the names as they can without looking in the Bible!

_____

_____

_____

_____

_____

_____

_____

_____

_____

_____

Many years before Christ's birth, which prophet said how Jesus would come?

Unscramble the letters to spell his name.

ASIIHA

The _____ will be with _____ and will give _____ to a _____ and will _____ him _____. Isaiah 7:14

Fill in the blanks.

Draw a line from each hat and pair of mittens to a child who needs them.

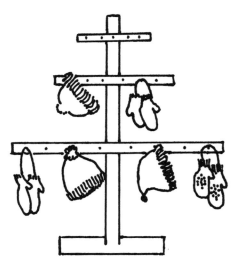

Because we have warm hearts we try to make warm hands—remember the mitten tree!

How many candles are left unlit? How many Sundays till Christmas?

BAPTISM

Elizabeth and Zechariah took baby John to the priest to give him to God. (Luke 1:59)

Parents today also bring their children to be baptized.

LISTEN: (What does our pastor say?)

"I baptize you in the name of the _____ and the _____ and the _____ _____."

CHILDREN'S BULLETIN

Draw the flames on the Advent candles that are lit.

MY SPIRIT REJOICES IN GOD MY SAVIOR!

Luke 1:47

BEHOLD
MEANS TO
LOOK!

Can you look and find which picture is different in each row?

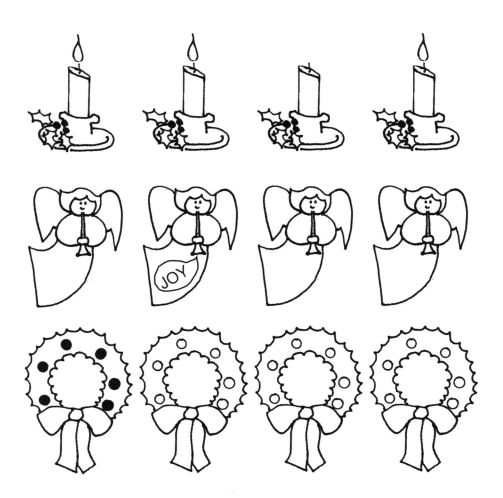

Draw in the flames

PREPARE REJOICE BEHOLD BELIEVE

LORD, SHINE IN OUR HEARTS AND LIVES

Luke 1:26-38

In each row circle the picture that is DIFFERENT.
Look in the Bible to answer the questions.

What is the name of the baby the angel announced? _____

What is the name of the angel who visited Mary? _____

Whose throne will God give to Jesus? _____

What town did Mary live in when the angel visited her?

_____

CHILDREN'S BULLETIN

Draw flames on the lighted candles. How many Sundays till Christmas?

THE WORD ANNOUNCED

Can you find the names hidden in the wreath? Write them below.

_____

_____

_____

When the angels had left them and gone into heaven, the shepherds said to one another, "Let's go to Bethlehem and see this thing that has happened, which the Lord has told us about."

Luke 2:15.

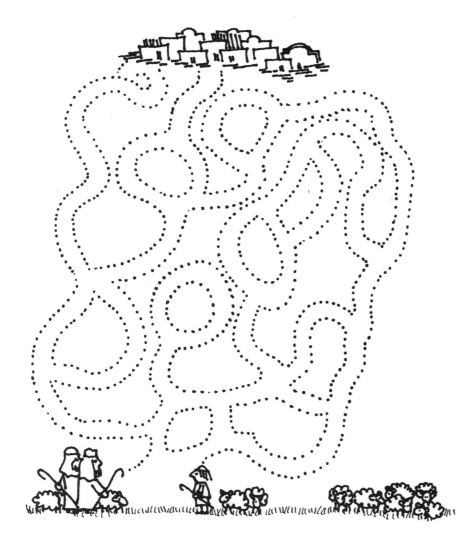

Help the shepherds find their way to Bethlehem.

Draw flames on the lighted candles. How many Sundays till Christmas?

THE WORD WELCOMED

Who were the first people to welcome Jesus? You'll find the answer hidden in the wreath.

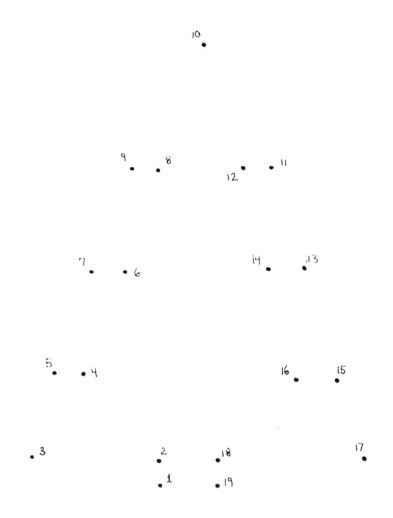

Decorate this tree with things that help you remember Christ's birth. Draw in . . .

- 🍬 for the shepherds who welcomed baby Jesus.
- 👼 for the angels who announced Christ's birth.
- ⭐ for the wisemen who worshiped the baby king.
- ♡ for God's great love to us!

Can you think of any other ornaments to add?

Can you unscramble the letters on the balls to find out what we're waiting for?

THE WORD
BECOMES
FLESH

"The Word became flesh" means that God became a human like us when Jesus was born.

Fill in the dotted squares to read the angel's message.

CHILDREN'S BULLETIN

Add the last flame to the candles—today is Christmas!

Color in all the letters F, L, P, X to read a special Christmas message.

Listen to the Sermon

Cross through each word as you hear the pastor say it.

Joseph	GOD	Child	Angel
Love	Mary	obedience	LORD
believe	son	JESUS	Nazareth
Egypt	Faith	Magi	dream

How many words can you make out of the letters in

BETHLEHEM?

_____

_____

_____

_____

Rearrange the letters on the Christmas balls to spell one of the names of Jesus. Write another name for Jesus on the long ribbon.

DRAW IN THE SHEPHERDS' FACES

First they were frightened.   Then they were glad.

WHICH WAY TO BETHLEHEM?

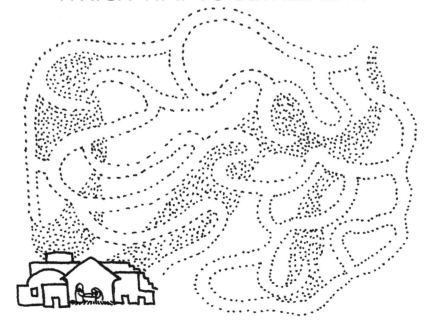

JESUS IS BORN. ALLELUIA!

Put the letters in the right order to spell what we do on Christmas.

Who surprised Mary with a visit?

Trace the path Mary took from her home to visit her cousin Elizabeth.

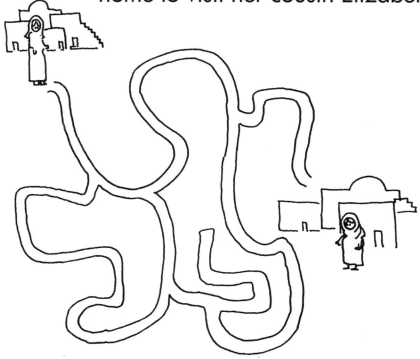

What did he tell her?

Happy is she who has believed that what God said he will do will be done!   Luke 1:45

(today's Bible word)

1 S	2 D	3 I	4 O	6 N	7 O	8 O	9 R	4 T	5 A	5 L	2 B
2 E	4 A	5 G	6 F	7 R	8 R	9 T	4 A	6 I	8 D	9 O	8 M
4 A	5 S	6 R	7 A	1 D	8 Y	2 Y	5 P	6 O	7 R	8 U	9 P
1 T	4 H	6 A	7 M	6 Y	7 O	8 E	9 T	2 F	4 O	1 P	6 U
2 N	3 O	4 D	5 T	7 O	8 F	2 A	3 H	4 Y	3 M	6 O	8 R
1 A	2 W	3 T	4 I	5 H	6 T	7 S	8 H	6 G	6 O	5 R	8 D

How did Mary feel when she first saw the angel?

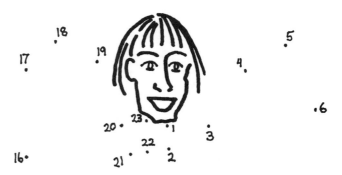

__ ___ ___

_____ , ____ ,

___ ____ _____

_____ ____ ____ .

The angel had a special message for Mary. To find out what it was, cross out all the odd numbers (1, 3, 5, 7, 9 are odd numbers). Put the rest of the letters in order in the blanks.

Who spoke to Joseph in his dreams?

Read Matthew 1 and 2. How many times does the angel of the Lord speak to Joseph in a dream? _____

What was the angel's first message to Joseph?

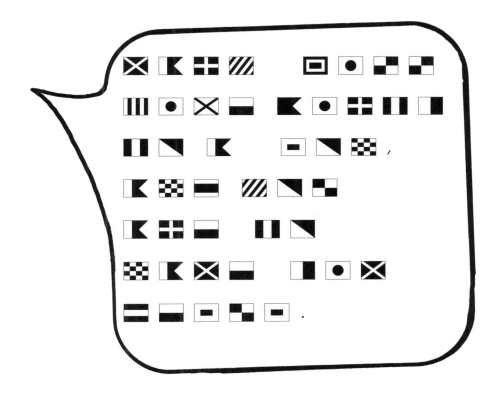

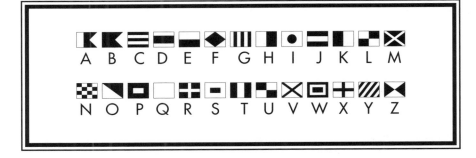

Draw in the faces of the heavenly host. What are they doing?

What did the angel say?

FIND THE WORDS

```
N  L  F  J  E  S  U  S  W
R  M  R  X  F  H  T  T  X
O  F  J  O  S  E  P  H  M
B  R  T  O  X  P  M  C  S
F  L  M  C  Y  H  L  B  Y
B  E  T  H  L  E  H  E  M
A  M  R  F  G  R  S  M  A
B  N  X  N  P  D  X  L  N
Y  M  A  R  Y  S  G  R  G
X  N  A  R  S  F  D  L  E
S  T  O  S  A  V  I  O  R
S  L  R  M  N  X  F  N  P
G  G  N  I  G  N  I  S  B
```

MARY	JOSEPH
JESUS	ANGEL
JOY	SHEPHERDS
GLORY	BETHLEHEM
SAVIOR	MANGER
BABY	STAR
SINGING	BORN

Find the hidden words:

GLORIFY   JOHN

MARY   REJOICE

SAVIOR   ZECHARIAH

ELIZABETH

PRAISE

BABY

JOY

```
L  R  P  X  S  S  F  N  Y  N
K  S  T  F  M  K  R  F  R  S
M  E  S  P  R  A  I  S  E  R
M  R  L  Q  N  R  M  P  B  Z
S  A  V  I  O  R  X  Y  A  A
X  L  S  L  Z  T  R  C  B  A
R  Y  G  B  X  A  W  L  Y  T
L  S  O  X  M  P  B  F  P  H
Q  R  E  J  O  I  C  E  X  Z
L  F  J  O  H  N  S  N  T  S
H  A  I  R  A  H  C  E  Z  H
```

Fill in the answers.

TUHR   ZBAO

DOBE

SESEJ

VADDI

POESJH   YRMA

Unscramble the names in Jesus' family tree.

If you were the innkeeper, how would you have answered Joseph's question, "Do you have room for us?" Draw the innkeeper at the door.

Help Mary and Joseph find a place to spend the night.

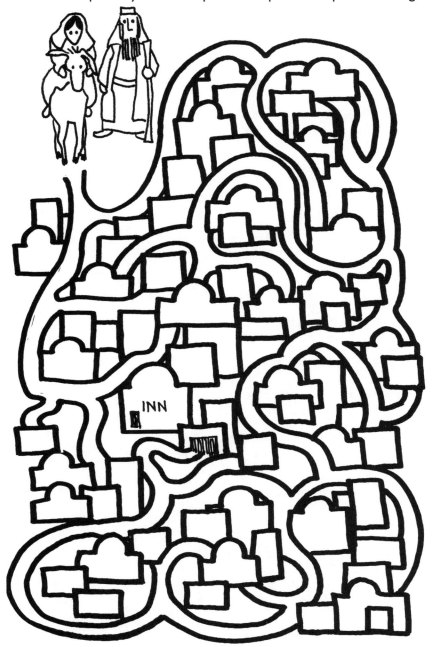

INN

Across

1. "Today in the town of David a _____ has been born." Luke 2:11
2. The city of David where Jesus was born.
4. Thre was no room there for Mary and Joseph to sleep.
5. Mary pondered everything here. (Luke 2:19)
6. They told the shepherds about Jesus' birth.

Down

1. The angels told them about Jesus' birth.
3. Jesus' first bed.

Another name for Bethlehem is the town of

__ __ __ __ __. (Luke 2:4)

Who is traveling to Bethlehem?

NAMES FOR JESUS

fill in the blanks.

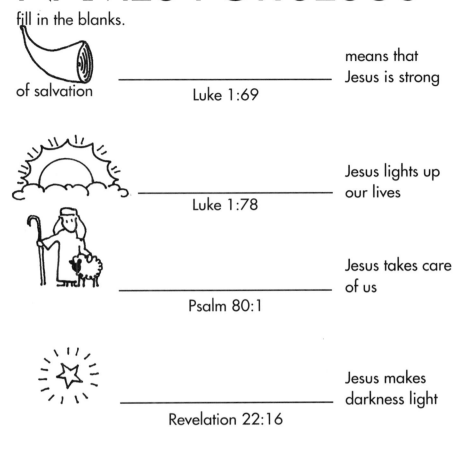

of salvation

_____ means that
Luke 1:69   Jesus is strong

_____ Jesus lights up
Luke 1:78   our lives

_____ Jesus takes care
Psalm 80:1   of us

_____ Jesus makes
Revelation 22:16   darkness light

IMMANUEL   God is with us

Matthew 1:23

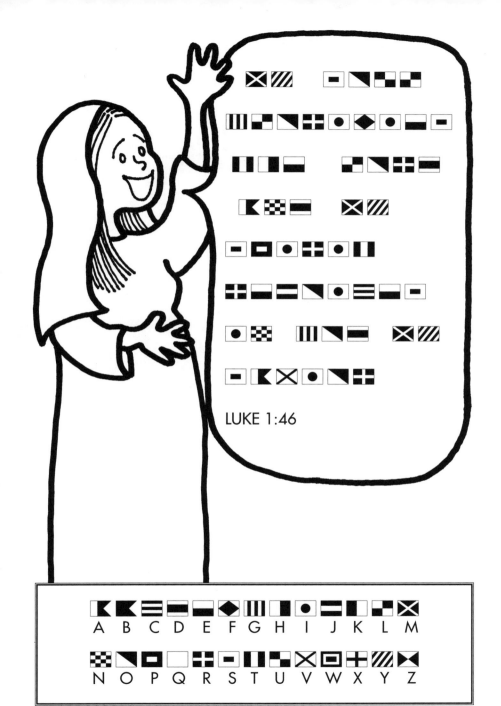

LUKE 1:46

Starting with the letter "T," use every other letter and go around twice to spell out the message.

Add straw to the manger for the baby Jesus.

___ ____

_____ _____

___ _____

_____

_____ __. John 1:14

To find out the angels' message, carefully fill in the dotted boxes.

How many angels are singing? _____
How many angels are playing musical instruments? _____
We don't really know if angels play harps or horns. But we do know that musical instruments are a great way to praise God. Write out the names of the people who played musical instruments in our church today:

WORD SEARCH LUKE 2:8–17

Twelve important words from Luke 2:8–17 are hidden below. How many can you find?

```
X  S  A  C  B  A  W  F  M
O  P  M  R  L  S  P  X  N
N  D  A  D  L  O  B  S  R
A  B  N  N  F  L  T  X  A
M  S  G  O  G  B  X  H  L
S  H  E  P  H  E  R  D  S
A  W  R  L  R  T  L  S  J
V  N  E  W  S  H  H  S  O
I  F  B  I  G  L  O  R  Y
O  X  R  A  X  E  S  X  L
R  H  Z  B  O  H  T  F  S
C  B  A  B  Y  E  N  O  N
L  A  C  F  X  M  N  B  Z
```

Glory to God in the highest

Can you find the angel who is different?

Help the shepherds find their way to the town of Bethlehem.

CHRISTMAS

The very first Christmas gift was from God. That gift was his son, Jesus.

Draw a picture of baby Jesus. Next, draw you beside the baby.

WORD SEARCH

Can you find the underlined words from the passage below in the mystery box?

"May the <u>grace</u> of the Lord <u>Jesus</u> <u>Christ</u>, and the <u>love</u> of God, and the <u>fellowship</u> of the <u>Holy</u> <u>Spirit</u> be with you <u>all</u>."
2 Corinthians 13:14

Mystery Box

```
O  W  W  T  G  S  X  D  A  Q  V  S
Q  E  A  Z  S  X  A  L  O  L  D  V
H  P  H  G  W  O  L  L  L  W  L  Q
K  W  F  G  I  Q  R  N  O  X  K  X
A  R  E  H  G  A  M  I  R  V  G  F
Q  F  L  W  V  V  L  L  O  G  E  D
X  K  L  O  G  R  A  C  E  I  K  S
Y  P  O  F  L  J  G  A  K  D  V  N
M  G  W  N  J  C  H  R  I  S  T  V
S  P  S  O  H  V  O  E  X  N  X  U
J  W  H  J  J  P  P  M  P  T  L  X
Y  B  I  O  Y  U  L  B  H  H  S  S
G  R  P  I  M  J  E  S  U  S  Z  B
Y  H  H  O  L  Y  S  P  I  R  I  T
I  T  D  D  E  L  W  A  R  H  E  Y
K  M  V  V  O  G  A  D  R  T  W  F
O  K  E  A  C  E  V  K  B  O  F  X
```

Christmas was last week. What do you do once you've celebrated Christ's birth? After they saw Jesus . . .

"the shepherds returned, glorifying and praising God for all the things they had heard and seen."
Luke 2:20

Draw the shepherd's happy face.

Not in a box,
not under the tree,
without a big bow,
came God's present to me.

Draw a Christmas picture below.

The church reformer Martin Luther loved evergreen trees because they reminded him of the everlasting life Christ brings! Can you find the Christmas words hidden in the tree?

_____

_____

_____

Which angel is different?

How many words can you make out of the letters in the name
SIMEON?

(The six we found are listed below. Can you find more?)

men, mine, sin, nose, no, me

_____

_____

_____

_____

_____

CHILDREN'S BULLETIN

Luke 2:21–40

When Jesus was eight days old, Mary and Joseph presented him at the temple. Two old people, Anna and Simeon, were very happy to see their Messiah. Simeon sang a song of praise about it.

Find twelve musical notes hidden in the picture.

Draw in Bethlehem so the wise men can find it!

SONG OF SIMEON

The 4th candle in the Advent Wreath is called "The Wise Men's Candle of Love."
Draw flames on the 4 small candles.

Draw a face on the baby.   Who is this baby?

John the Baptist saw Jesus.
What did he say?
(John 1:29)

Carefully color the shapes with dots in them.

Today we'll learn about

SIN

What a scary thought!

Even great men of God had to be forgiven. Do you know who these men are?

Wow! God could still love and forgive him after THAT!

But remember, Jesus died to pay for your sins. He WANTS to forgive us!

The great letter writer once persecuted Christians. (Acts 21:40–22:5)

This man lied about his wife. (Genesis 12; 17:5)

Jesus called him "the rock," but this disciple denied him three times. (Matthew 26:69–75)

God helped him kill a giant, but he had a man killed and stole his wife. (2 Samuel 12:9–12)

This man made a golden calf for the people to worship. (Exodus 32)

He led the people out of Egypt but he didn't follow God's directions. (Numbers 20:7–12)

CHILDREN'S BULLETIN

After John baptized Jesus, the Holy Spirit led him into the wilderness.

In the wilderness, Jesus prayed and Satan tempted him.

JOURNEY TO THE CROSS

JOURNEY INTO THE WILDERNESS

Matthew 4:1–11

The journey into the wilderness was the first part of Jesus' journey to the cross to die for our sins.

What is a JOURNEY? (circle one)

a trip

a flower

a singing group

What is THE WILDERNESS? (circle one)

a big store

a mountain

wild land where no people live

What is TEMPTATION? (circle one)

a perfume

a dessert

thinking about doing something wrong

Satan tried to tempt Jesus to do wrong three times. Draw a picture of each thing he wanted Jesus to do.

Matthew 4:3–4

Matthew 4:5–7

Matthew 4:8–10

Jesus' disciples got hungry as they walked through a wheat field on the Sabbath day. They picked some grain and ate it. This upset some Pharisees. But Jesus said it was all right.

Who is the "LORD OF THE SABBATH"?

(Matthew 12:8) Can you find it hidden in the grain?)

"Son of Man" is one of Matthew's favorite titles for Jesus. Of course, he is also the Son of God.

Sabbath = God's special Old Testament day
What did he do? (See Genesis 2:1–2.) _____

Sunday = God's special New Testament day
What did he do? (See Mark 16:9.) _____

The Sabbath (and Sunday for us) should be days we DO things. Find the the thing Jesus told the Pharisees in Matthew 12:12 that they should do.

Circle in the letters below the good things to do every day.

MATTHEW 6:5-8

In some places in the world people have liked to show off by making loud, long prayers where everyone could see them. These were the **hypocrites** Jesus was talking about (Matthew 6:5). These hypocrites weren't really trying to speak to God, they were trying to show off to men with their prayers.

Our prayers need to be **LARE.**
(Unscramble the letters.)

___ ___ ___ ___

To help his disciples understand about real prayer, Jesus told them a story that Luke wrote down. You can read the story in Luke 18:9–14. Which man's prayer was real?

THE LORD'S PRAYER
Matthew 6:9–13

```
T  Y  L  I  A  D  Y  O  U
E  B  R  E  V  I  L  E  D  D
M  R  R  E  H  T  A  F  I  I
P  H  T  R  A  E  O  Z  U  U
T  N  D  A  E  R  B  I  N  N
A  E  L  E  G  O  I  N  A  A
T  M  K  I  N  G  D  O  M  M
I  A  V  A  R  L  I  V  E  E
O  E  V  I  G  W  I  L  L  L
N  D  B  N  E  V  A  E  H
```

Can you find these hidden words which are from the prayer Jesus taught his disciples in Matthew 6?

BE	WILL	HEAVEN
IN	KINGDOM	BREAD
FORGIVE	DELIVER	FATHER
GIVE	TEMPTATION	DAILY
AMEN	NAME	EARTH
EVIL		

THSER EKSIBNAGODGOOMZ OTORF RHEESZAXVVEQN ITSO VLEISKPE TRHJIKST

Fill in the dotted letters to read the title.

How did the king feel?
What did he do?

What does this story mean for us?

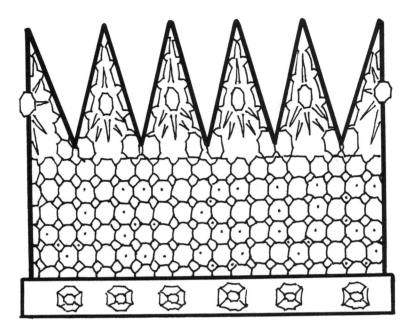

Color in the dotted jewels on the crown to see the name of our King.
Write His name in the jewel below.

The kingdom of heaven is like a mustard seed, which a man took and planted in his field.

Though it is the smallest of all your seeds, yet when it grows, it is the largest of garden plants and becomes a tree, so that the birds of the air come and perch in its branches.
Matthew 13:31–32

Can you find all ten birds perched in the mustard plant's branches?

These men want to carry their friend to Jesus. Can you help them find their way?

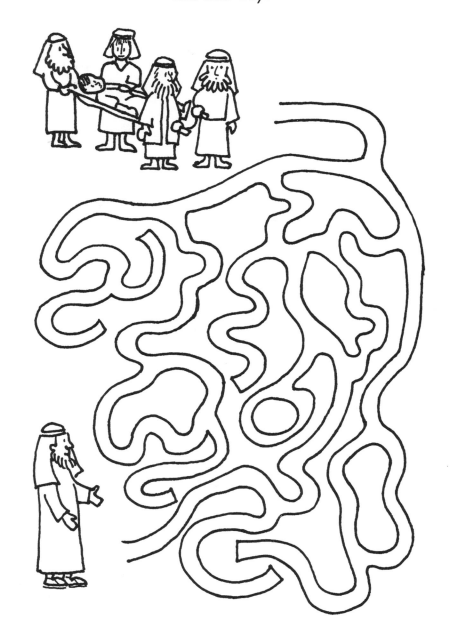

Some men carried their friend to Jesus. Can you circle the things you can carry?

Decode Jesus' message.

How did Jesus answer his disciple's question? (See Matthew 19:26)

How can anyone be saved, then?!

How many of Jesus' twelve disciples can you find in this word maze? See Luke 6:14–16 for their names.

```
T N H O J J T T G P Y K
X N V S S D A M M A A W
A Y H A L A A M S F J E
R G K C N T M A E B J M
S H L G T D D O N S P O
I W Y H L U R A H F U L
G Y E I J L K E P T W O
O W S I M O N X W Y O H
A M T P H I L I P Q U T
D U C P E T E R W X O R
B Y H W Y W J B J A Y A
W S O M P B G M R F F B
```

A B C D E F G H I J K L M N O P Q R S T U V W X Y Z

MATTHEW 9:1–8 TREASURE HUNT

1. Who rode in a  ?

2. Who carried  ?

3. What was forgiven?

4. Who had evil thoughts in their ♡ ?

5. Who was told to "Get up, pick up his 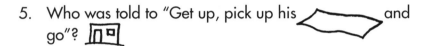 and go"? 🏠

6. Who was filled with awe?

TAWETMH

__ __ __ __ __ __ __

Unscramble the letters to know for a fact the name of the man who wrote down Jesus' acts. He collected taxes and had a bad name, but Jesus chose him just the same.

(To read about his own story, read chapter 9:9–13.)

CHILDREN'S BULLETIN

THE CROWD WAS FILLED WITH

Matthew 9:1–8

Why? What does AWE mean?
Awe = a strong feeling of respect, fear, and wonder.
Can you draw their faces to show their awe?

Jesus sent out seventy-two disciples "two by two" to go into every town and place he planned to visit.
What were they supposed to do?
(See Luke 10:9.)

Can you match the disciples that are exactly alike?

The _____ is _____, but the workers are few. Ask the _____ of the _____ to send out _____ into his _____ field.

Luke 10:2

Which pair of disciples is dressed the way Jesus wanted them to be for their trip? (See Luke 10:4.)

Connect the dots below to see the kind of crown the cheering crowd thought Jesus would wear.

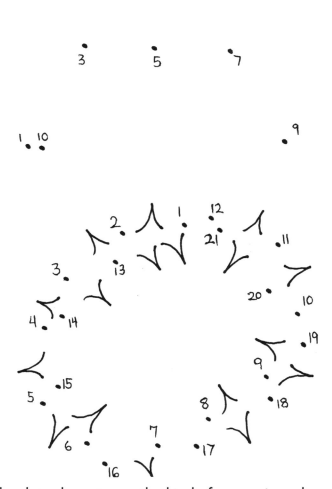

Connect the dots above to see the kind of crown Jesus knew he soon would wear.

Draw palm branches for all the children to wave. Why are they so excited?

Palm Sunday Hymn

All Glory, Laud, and Honor

Look how this song has grown! Think how many Christians have sung this to God as you are singing today!

 The words are 1100 years old.

The tune is over 375 years old.

 The harmony is 266 years old.

This translation is nearly 150 years old.

Draw you and your family singing it today.

CHILDREN'S BULLETIN

Fill in the dotted squares.

Crossword Puzzle

Luke 19:28-40

CHILDREN'S BULLETIN

Across

3. What did the disciples put on the road and on Jesus' donkey?
4. The city Jesus rode into.
5. If the people kept quiet, what would cry out in praise?
7. What did Jesus ride on?

Down

1. What the Pharisees called Jesus.
2. Who complained about the cheering crowd?
6. How many disciples did Jesus send before him to the village?

What did the children wave? Draw one in this boy's hand.

Finish decorating the letters of HOSANNA!

Three of these people are missing their palm branches. Can you draw them in?

Matthew 21 Crossword Puzzle

Across
2. The city Jesus rode into (Matthew 21:1).
3. What the people shouted (Matthew 21:9).
4. A Bible word that means "happy" (Matthew 21:9).
6. The crowds cheered Jesus because they thought he was a new _____ (Matthew 21:5).

Down
1. Jesus rode on this animal (Matthew 21:7).
2. The man the people cheered.
5. They called him Son of _____ (Matthew 21:9).

Children's Bulletin

Draw in the happy faces of the children who are praising Jesus.

Find the underlined words in the scrambled-word box below.

Thursday was a very hard day for <u>Jesus</u>. He went with his <u>disciples</u> to Jerusalem to eat the special <u>Passover</u> meal. But when they went into the room where they were going to eat, no one was ready to <u>wash</u> their dirty <u>feet</u>. The disciples argued about this, but Jesus knelt down and washed their feet himself!

When they ate the Passover meal, Jesus told his friends that the <u>bread</u> was his body and the <u>wine</u> his blood. The disciples didn't understand this. Then he told them that one of them would <u>betray</u> him. They were <u>surprised</u> and shocked. But Judas left to tell Jesus' <u>enemies</u> where he was.

Jesus and the other disciples sang a <u>hymn</u> and then went to a nearby garden. Jesus was sad and upset, and he <u>prayed</u> late into the night. His disciples fell asleep. Then <u>Judas</u>, followed by Jesus' enemies, came. They captured him, and all the rest of the disciples ran away.

```
R Q J D J Y D A E R B F F
P D L I E E W E N I W E H
A E E S T U S V D X P Y N
S S K C S F A U A F M S B
S I L I E E D Q S N O E W
O R H P I E U J Y H T D A
V P T L M T J A N R Q U S
E R Y E E V U R A N T N H
R U O S N E W Y O H W M W
U S X B E B D E Y A R P K
```

CHILDREN'S BULLETIN

EAT MY . . .

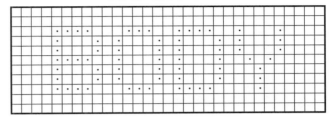

DRINK MY . . .

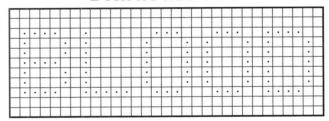

What would you have felt if you heard those words?

gross!

What does THAT mean?

Hey! That isn't part of the Passover ritual!

Where is Judas going?

Fill in the dotted squares to read what Jesus said.

Draw the food on the table: meat, thin bread, and wine. Draw the faces of Jesus' disciples.

The disciples ate and remembered how God had rescued the Israelites from Egypt. The blood of a lamb on the door had saved them from the angel of death. Jesus knew that in a few hours he would die as the LAMB OF GOD. His blood saves us from death!

God uses two special meals to help his people remember what he has done for them.

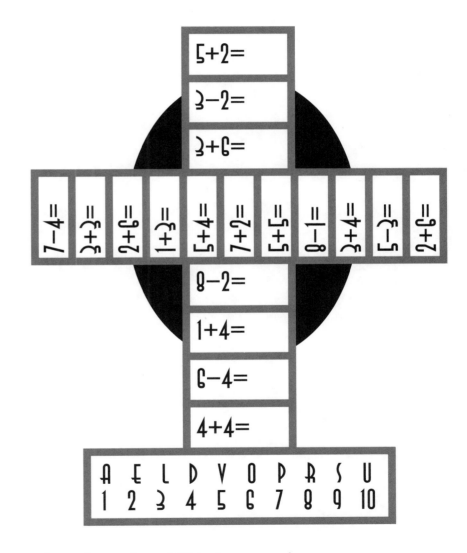

Work out the math and fill in the proper letters.

How many different words can you make using the letters in the word

RESURRECTION?

_____

_____

_____

_____

_____

_____

10 words = good!
20 words = great!
30 words = super!

Can you find the two lilies that are exactly the same? How many pots of Easter lilies can you see in church today? _____

Children's Bulletin

Easter morning started with a lot of frightened people. Why are these soldiers scared? Who else was afraid early this day? (See Matthew 28.)

Listen to the Sermon

Put an X over each word you hear the pastor say.

✝ JESUS	VICTORY!	Believe	New 
Lazarus	NOW	Jordan River	ETERNITY
Understand	Bethany	Safety	I AM
LIFE	Martha	Resurrection	Christ
Abundant	♥ Love	Raised	♥ Hearts ♥

Can you find the one egg that is different?

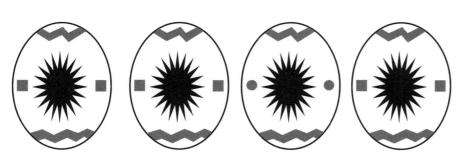

What did the angel tell the startled women?
Fill in the speech bubble.

"There was a violent earthquake, for an angel of the Lord came down from heaven and, going to the tomb, rolled back the stone. . . . The guards were so afraid of him that they shook and became like dead men." Matthew 28:2, 4

Draw a stunned guard below the angel.

Children's Bulletin

Try to thank a trumpeter after church.

Color the letters so that it's easy to see why we're excited today! Count the trumpets on this page. How many trumpeters are playing in our church today?

Fill in the blanks.
What did Christ's death and resurrection do for us?

. . . just as _____ was _____ from the
_____ through the glory of the _____, we
too may _____ a new _____!
(See Romans 6:4.)

Easter is a celebration of Christ's

_ _ _ _ _ _ _ _ _ _ _ _ _

Can you find the letters of this word hidden in the Easter egg?

CHILDREN'S BULLETIN

What question did the angels ask the women at the tomb? (See Luke 24:5.)

Help these friends of Jesus find their way to the tomb.

What are some words to describe how the friends of Jesus felt as they went to the tomb the first Easter morning? _____

_____

What did the angel say?

What are some words to describe how the friends of Jesus felt after they heart the angel's message?

_____

Connect the dots.

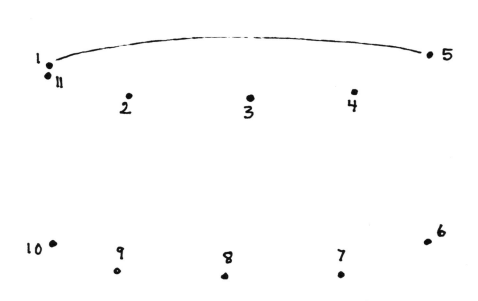

Today Is the Birthday of
THE CHURCH

Draw as many lighted candles as you can fit on the cake. The church is nearly 2,000 years old!

Suddenly a sound like the blowing of a mighty wind came from heaven and filled the whole house

What is happening? What did the disciples see appearing on each other's heads? (See Acts 2) Draw them on.

Miscellaneous

Baptism
The Lord's Supper
Prayer
Pauline Epistles
Seasonal

What Is God Telling Us with His Signs?

Look at the signs. Write the word that . . .

1. begins with Y and ends with U _____

2. begins with A and ends with E _____

3. begins with M and ends with Y _____

4. begins with P and ends with E _____

GOD'S SIGN LANGUAGE

Word Search

Find the underlined words from the story in the scrambled-word box below.

A stranger walked to Emmaus with two disciples after Jesus' death. They were sad and confused, but the stranger explained to them why Jesus had to die. They asked him to stop for supper. When the stranger thanked God for the food, the men recognized him. It was Jesus! He was alive!

```
E I G E A Z E C D E W V
E M M A U S Q T N I P Z
U S B I A Y C Z B Z A S
E E A K I X Z X E P Y T
E L T C C F S O G F F R
X P C O N F U S E D N A
R I A T H A N K E D K N
U C B D M M A Y V A G G
F S I F N Y D D O G G E
M I W W A L I V E L P R
M D U F D K I H T A E D
J E S U S A W D O O F S
W W F R Y G S R B Y R K
```

CHILDREN'S BULLETIN

The adults may be serious and the music may be quiet, but communion is still a celebration! How many different words can you make out of the word **CELEBRATION?**

_____

_____

_____

I baptise you in the name of
_____ and the
_____ and the
_____ _____

fill in the blanks

Help the family find
their way to the
baptism font.

CHILDREN'S BULLETIN

Connect the dots. Who must work in our hearts for us to be saved?

9.
3.
2.
.8
10.   4.
7.   1.
5.   29
11.   28
6.
12.   .26
13.   27   25   24
14.   .19
15.   .20
16. 17 18   23
21   22

To refuse to let the Holy Spirit work in our hearts means we refuse God. What does Jesus call it? See Matthew 12:31.

What are our hearts like without God? Fill in the heart so that it is dark—but leave the dove white.

When Jesus first gave the wine and bread to the disciples, he said it was to remind them of his gift of salvation. Color in the dotted spaces in the heart and you will find something else that reminds us of his great gift to us.

COMMUNION

IS A SPECIAL MEAL FOR GOD AND HIS FAMILY.

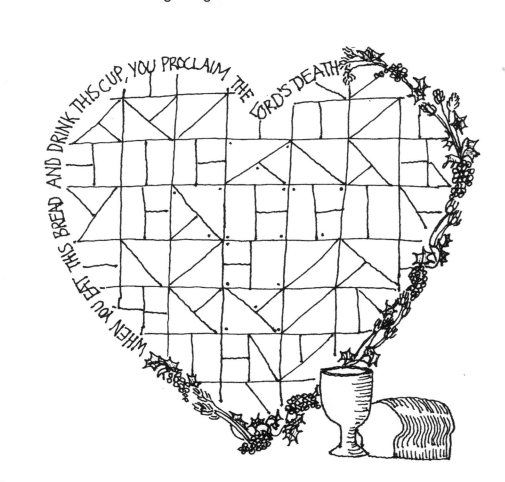

How do grapes and stalks of wheat remind us of the bread and wine of the Lord's Supper?

Can you find the letters that spell LORD'S SUPPER hidden in the picture?

Can you find the underlined words in the scrambled-word box below?

The Lord <u>Jesus</u>, on the night he was betrayed, took <u>bread</u>, and when he had given <u>thanks</u>, he broke it and said,
"This is my <u>body</u>, which is for you; do this to <u>remember</u> me."
In the same way, after supper he took the <u>cup</u>, saying,
"This cup is the new <u>covenant</u> in my <u>blood</u>; <u>drink</u> it to remember me."
Whenever you <u>eat</u> this bread and drink this cup, you proclaim the Lord's <u>death</u> until he comes. (See 1 Corinthians 11:23–26.)

If you hear the pastor say these words today, draw a smile on this face. ☺

```
J T N A N E V O C T A E H
C H O F N E O B S O D O S
D L E F C C P X Z C G Z I
O E K O L L V Y W E J E A
O E U N R E B M E M E R P
L V F B I A W T J Z A T X
B X B Q H R C S U S E J F
I T T I U T D C Z D Q V T
S Z H B D J A F F C U P O
B P W A M K K E F B V H M
M J E F N E W C D Q O X X
H R D W F K N J T Z J D L
B C E I G R S T T D N L Y
```

Help the family find their way to the baptism font.

Who was baptized today?

Fill in dotted shapes to see what is served at the communion table of the Lord's Supper.

LORD'S SUPPER MYSTERY

BEFORE THE LORD'S SUPPER WE EXAMINE OUR HEARTS & OUR LIVES...WE DO NOT MEASURE UP!

BUT GOD'S GRACE HELPS US PREPARE OUR HEARTS!

CHILDREN'S BULLETIN

OUR FATHER IN HEAVEN
IINIIO WID
BE YOUR NAME

Add horizontal lines (they go this _____ way) to the broken letters above to see what Jesus said.

WE PRAY IN DIFFERENT WAYS

Put an **X** in a box each time we pray silently in church today.
Put an **O** in a box each time we pray through a song.
Put an **!** in a box each time we read a printed prayer together.
Put a △ in a box each time the pastor leads our prayers.
Put a † in a box each time we pray some other way.

Many Christians raise their hands when they pray. This helps us remember to praise God in our prayers.

Many Christians kneel when they pray. This reminds us to be humble before God.

Sometimes Christians hold hands when they pray. This reminds us that God has united us into his family.

How do YOU use your body when you pray? Draw a picture here.

- Can you find the hidden letters to spell out the name of the person who taught us to pray?
- Decorate the outlined letters and color the picture.

PRAYER

is _____

(Fill in the blank with what you think prayer is.)

What do we pray for and about?

Draw pictures in each box of what you could pray for.

I am thankful for . . .

I am worried about . . .

People . . .

I can praise God . . .

When we pray, we talk to God. How does God talk to us? He speaks to us using the . . .

Bible and our ♥

Famous Bible Prayers

Do you know the Bible people who prayed these prayers? Try the crossword with the clues first; use the Bible verse only if you're stumped.

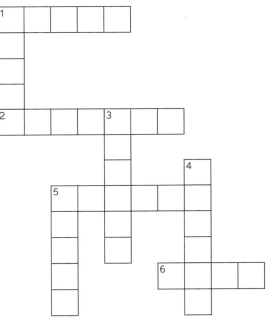

Across

1. He prayed from inside a great fish (Jonah 2:1–2).
2. He was the first Christian to be killed for his faith. He prayed that God would forgive his killers (Acts 7:59–60).
5. Because he prayed every day, he was thrown to the lions in Babylon (Daniel 6:10–12).
6. Her prayer praises God for sending Jesus as her Savior as well as her son (Luke 1:46–55).

Down

1. When he prayed on the Mount of Olives before his death, his sweat fell like great drops of blood (Luke 22:39–44).
3. A priest who saw her praying thought she was drunk. She was praying for a baby (1 Samuel 1:10–11).
4. When he prayed, God sent fire that burned up his offering, the stone altar, and the water around it (1 Kings 18:36–39).
5. Many of the Psalms were the prayers of this great king (Psalm 65).

What do we call the prayer Jesus taught his disciples?

Christians all over the world use this prayer.
DID YOU NOTICE? Did we use this prayer in our morning worship service? _____

Our <u>Father</u> in <u>heaven</u>, hallowed be your <u>name</u>, your <u>kingdom</u> come, your will be done on <u>earth</u> as it is in heaven. Give us <u>today</u> our daily <u>bread</u>. Forgive us our debts as we <u>forgive</u> our debtors. And lead us not into temptation, but deliver us from <u>evil</u>.
Matthew 6:9–13

Can you find the underlined words from the prayer in the scrambled-word box?

PRAYER

```
Q H C F X K Z P
B K R T D I B D
X U H B K N F B
Y B W Y F G F E
V H O M A D U A
D B Q D T O L R
X Y K A H M I T
A W L C E O V H
K G V P R B E C
U O Q E Y O H L
E U T V N B P N
M E J I V H P E
A I B G J Y O V
N K B R F Y T A
K Y S O H O B E
J B V F D N L H
A Z D A C B C C
W O Y S Z I I U
V A Z D A E R B
```

Color the leaves that have dots in them.

"Growing in the Lord" means we need to work to be the sort of children God wants.

HARDER STUFF: What fruits grow on your spiritual tree? Check Galatians 5:22–23 for some ideas.

Can you find two matching things in each row?

Do you know what Bible story I come from?

Remember: It is not always easy to forgive. It is not easy for God either. He had to DIE to forgive us.

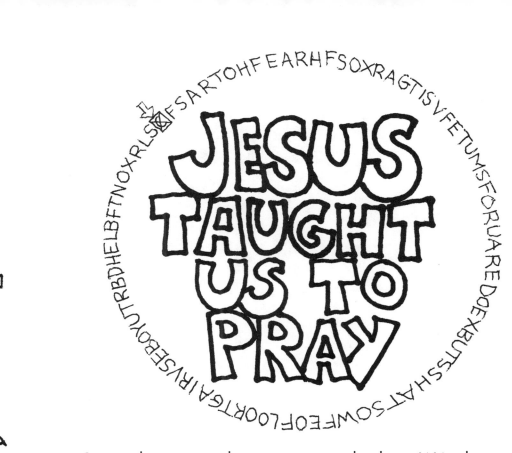

Start at the arrow and cross out every other letter. Write the remaining letters in the blanks below.

F_ _ _ _ _ _ ... _ _ _ _ _ _ _ _

_ _ _ _ _ _ _ _ _ _ _ _ _ _

_ _ _ _ _ _ _ _ _ _ _

_ _ _ _ _ _ _ _ _ _ _ _ .

Matthew 6:12 KJV

Our Father who is in heaven,
HALLOWED be your name.

How do we keep God's name "hallowed"?

1. Like the writer
of Psalm 145,
we can praise
God's name.

I WILL PRAISE YOUR NAME...

How long did the psalm-singer want to praise God's name? Fill in the rest of this sentence. Psalm 145:1

2. We can be careful never
to use God's name carelessly.
We must use his name only
when we mean to speak to
him or talk about him.

3. We must be careful how we behave. As CHRISTians, we carry
one of God's names. We need to act like his children.

Some of God's Names

Across

1. Jesus taught us to call God this when we pray.
(Matthew 6:9)
4. Another word for a ruler. (Psalm 145:3)
5. Jesus is this. (John 1:41)
7. Because God is our ruler we call him this. (Psalm 145:1)
8. Jesus is God and Jesus is the _____. (Matthew 1:16)

Down

2. A special "cozy" word for father in the language of Jesus'
first disciples. (Romans 8:15)
3. Because God is strong, we call him this. (Psalm 144:1).
4. When John saw Jesus he called him this. (John 1:29)
6. Because God saves us he is this. (Psalm 68:19).

Jesus told his disciples: "The Kingdom of God is not over here or over there; it is within you."
(See Luke 17:21)

Find your way to the children in the center of the maze.

CHILDREN'S BULLETIN

YOUR KINGDOM COME

God's Kingdom begins in our hearts when Jesus rules as King there.

Jesus offered the Samaritan woman living water (if you don't know the story, ask your parents). She was so excited that she forgot her water jug and ran back to the village. Which of these water jugs matches hers?

YOUR WILL BE DONE ON EARTH AS IT IS IN HEAVEN

Connect the dots.

Follow the lines to see where these Christian children live.

GIVE US TODAY OUR DAILY BREAD

Can you find two matching things in each row?

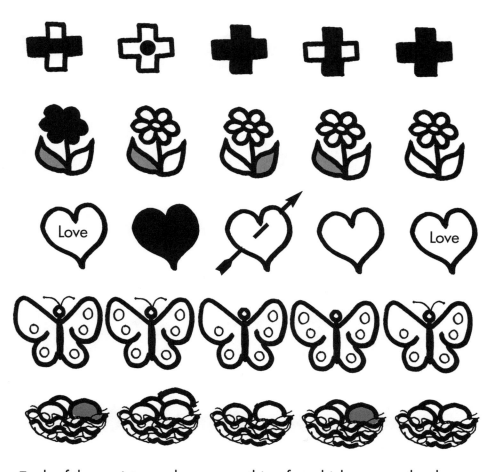

Each of these pictures shows something for which we can thank OUR FATHER when we pray. Draw five other things you are thankful for.

God has many different names in the Bible. Sometimes we call him Lord or Jehovah. Which name did Jesus teach us to use when we pray? (Fill in the dotted squares.)

THINK ABOUT THE MUSIC

Color the instruments you hear today.

Sing to Praise!

Sing to Pray!

Draw yourself singing.

You Are an Agent with a SPECIAL MISSION.

(Decode the message to find out about it!)

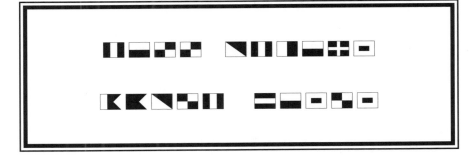

This Sunday has a special name. What is it?

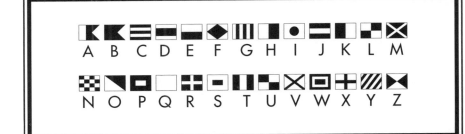

In Jesus' name, Peter healed a beggar who had never walked!
Draw SURPRISED

and HAPPY

faces on the man.

He walked, leaped, and praised God!

THERE IS NO OTHER NAME... BY WHICH WE MUST BE SAVED!
(Acts 4:12)

Fill in the dotted shapes.

This African was an important servant to the queen of Ethiopia. Draw on the clothes and jewels such a man would wear.

HARDER STUFF: (Read Acts 8:26–39.)

    1. Who is this man? _____

    2. Why is he confused? _____

    3. What will Philip tell him? _____

Draw in happy faces.

They could be singing or laughing or . . . ?

The angel sent Philip down the road to meet a stranger. Can you help him meet up with the African man?

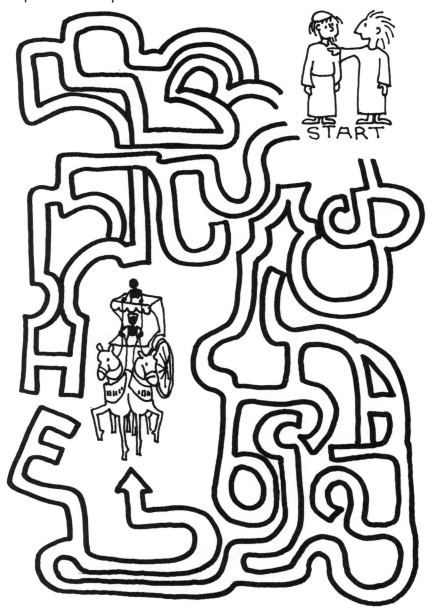

Can you find the hidden word?

Listen to the Sermon

Mark an X through each word you hear the pastor say during his sermon today.

8 words = good, 10 words = great, 15 words = super!

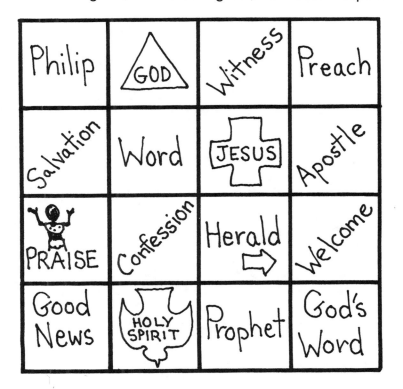

Philip	GOD	Witness	Preach
Salvation	Word	JESUS	Apostle
PRAISE	Confession	Herald	Welcome
Good News	HOLY SPIRIT	Prophet	God's Word

Bible-time believers read the Word of God from SCROLLS, not books. Can you find two scrolls that are the same?

EARLY CHRISTIAN FELLOWSHIP
Acts 2:42–47

How did the early Christians act? Read Acts 2:42–47. Put an X over the pictures which are NOT what the early Christians did.

We Worship God in Many Different Ways

How many songs did we sing this morning?

How many times did we pray in church today?

What was the title of today's sermon? _____

What was today's offering for? (Check the adult bulletin.) _____

How many people played instruments in church today?

Which book in the Bible did we read from today? _____

AND THE GIFT GOES ON...  ...AND THE GIFT GOES ON...  ...AND THE GIFT GOES ON...

FREELY YOU HAVE RECEIVED, FREELY GIVE

Matthew 10:8

How can YOU share the gift? Draw pictures in the gift boxes.

FAMOUS BIBLE FATHERS

Match the names to the fathers below.

ABRAHAM   ZECHARIAH

JESSE   ADAM

JOSEPH   DAVID

My youngest son killed a giant and later became Israel's king.

I was ready to sacrifice my son at God's command.

I was the first father. To my sorrow, one son murdered another.

My son was also my savior! He was born in a Bethlehem stable.

My son was Israel's wisest king.

An angel came to me in the temple to say I would have a son!

CHILDREN'S BULLETIN

LOVE THE LORD YOUR GOD WITH ALL YOUR HEART AND SOUL AND STRENGTH
(see Deuteronomy 6:5.)

Draw YOUR father talking to these children. Add yourself too!

Isaiah 65:17–25 Crossword Puzzle

What will the new heaven and the new earth be like?

Across

3. While his people are still speaking, God promises to do this (verse 24).
4. This animal will eat straw (verse 25).
5. The sound of this will not be heard (verse 19).
6. What the lion will eat (verse 25).

Down

1. God will answer before his people do this (verse 24).
2. What they will do to vineyards (verse 21).
3. God will create a new earth and new _____ (verse 17).
5. He will eat with the lamb (verse 25).

Can you find the two lions that are the same?

Revelation 21 talks about the new heaven and earth.

Draw in the happy faces of God's people.

Start with the letter under the arrow, and write down every other letter to read how Revelation 21 describes the new earth.

___ ___ ___ ___   ___ ___ ___ ___ ___ ___

___ ___   ___ ___ ___   ___ ___ ___ ___

___ ___ ___ ___ .   ___ ___ ___ ___ ___

___ ___ ___ ___ ___ ___   ___ ___ ___

___ ___ ___ ___ ___ ___ ___ .

Be devoted to one another
in brothery love.

Romans 12:10

Who's showing devotion and brotherly love? Circle the pictures.

To be **DEVOTED** is to have an on-going, long-term love that does not change.

Draw a picture of how YOU can show brotherly love or devotion
to other Christians this week.

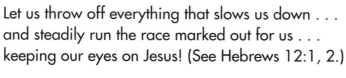

Let us throw off everything that slows us down . . . and steadily run the race marked out for us . . . keeping our eyes on Jesus! (See Hebrews 12:1, 2.)

Clouds of Witnesses

The author of Hebrews says we're running our race in front of an audience—the men and women who died loving the Lord. Can you find these famous believers?

What things did this runner throw off to run her fastest for Jesus? Is there anything *you* should throw off?

Across

2. God's strong man. He wasn't supposed to cut his hair. (Judges 13)
5. This brave woman helped Israelite spies escape from Jericho. (Joshua 2)
6. His jealous brother murdered him. (Genesis 4).

Down

1. As a boy in the temple, God called his name. (1 Samuel 3)
3. He sailed an ark in a huge flood. (Genesis 6)
4. This shepherd boy became king of Israel. (1 Samuel 16:10–13)

Who Said Good-bye?

Look up each verse. Draw a line from the circled verse to the name of the person who said good-bye.

Paul—The Great Church-Planter

Acts 13–28 is all about Paul's missionary trips and the churches that he started. Acts 20 is the story of Paul saying good-bye to one church he started. Everybody was sad, but churches don't depend on one leader or missionary. Who is the REAL leader of the church?

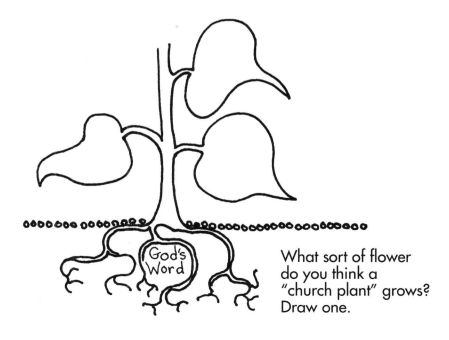

What sort of flower do you think a "church plant" grows? Draw one.

DO NOT BE ANXIOUS ABOUT ANYTHING

BUT IN EVERYTHING, BY PRAYER AND PETITION

WITH THANKSGIVING, PRESENT YOUR REQUESTS TO GOD

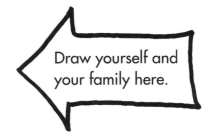

Draw yourself and your family here.

AND THE PEACE OF GOD WILL GUARD YOUR HEARTS...

Draw sad faces in the top row
and happy faces in the bottom row.

PRAISE BE TO THE GOD AND FATHER OF
OUR LORD JESUS CHRIST . . . THE GOD
OF ALL COMFORT

Beginning with the letter "G"
write down every other letter in
the spaces below.

___ _____ __ __

____ ___ _____, __

____ __ ___ _____

____ ___ _____

____ ___. _____. 1:3–4

Color each word
you hear the
pastor say.

Can you find which stem leads to the flower?

CHILDREN'S BULLETIN

Look in the grown-ups' bulletin to find the title for today's sermon. Write it in the box below. Then listen carefully when the pastor reads the Bible and talks. Draw a picture to go along with the sermon.

The Bible is not the only way God teaches us about himself. Fill the vowels in the blanks below to read how the Belgic Confession explains it.

A=1	E=2	I=3	O=4	U=5

TH__ W__RLD __S B__F__R__
1+1   6−2   7−4   5−3   3+1   2−0

__ __R __Y__S L__K__ __
8−4   3+2   6−4   1+1   6−3   11−9   9−8

B__ __T F__L B__ __K __N
5−3   1+0   7−2   1+2   11−6   3+1   7−3   4−1

WH__CH __LL CR__ __T__R__S,
3+0   2−1   10−8   5−4   3+2   1+1

GR__ __T __ND SM__LL, H__LP
3−1   6−5   1+0   10−9   1+1

__S T__ R__M__MB__R __ND
9−4   3+1   3−1   6−4   1+1   7−6

GL__R__FY G__D.
3+1   7−4   2+2

WORD SEARCH

Can you find these words which help to describe God?

What Is God Like?

```
U  N  C  H  A  N  G  E  A  B  L  E
E  E  L  B  I  S  I  V  N  I  U  M
R  K  X  Q  G  Q  M  L  C  B  F  D
C  W  C  N  A  L  M  I  G  H  T  Y
Q  T  H  C  F  X  Z  W  P  B  K  A
T  S  D  B  E  T  I  N  I  F  N  I
D  U  X  U  H  B  K  F  B  S  Y  B
W  J  Y  E  T  E  R  N  A  L  E  F
V  H  O  M  U  D  B  Q  D  X  Y  K
A  A  W  L  C  O  K  G  V  P  B  C
G  O  O  D  U  O  Q  Y  O  H  L  U
```

☐ ALMIGHTY   ☐ ETERNAL   ☐ GOOD   ☐ INFINITE
☐ INVISIBLE   ☐ JUST   ☐ UNCHANGEABLE   ☐ WISE

God is with us wherever we go.

Draw some happy faces.

SCHOOL IS STARTING

CHILDREN'S BULLETIN

Follow the trails. Who goes to WHICH school? What school school do *you* go to?

and know that I AM GOD

Fill in the dotted shapes to read God's message.

CHILDREN'S BULLETIN

Can you find the two pictures that are ALIKE in each row?

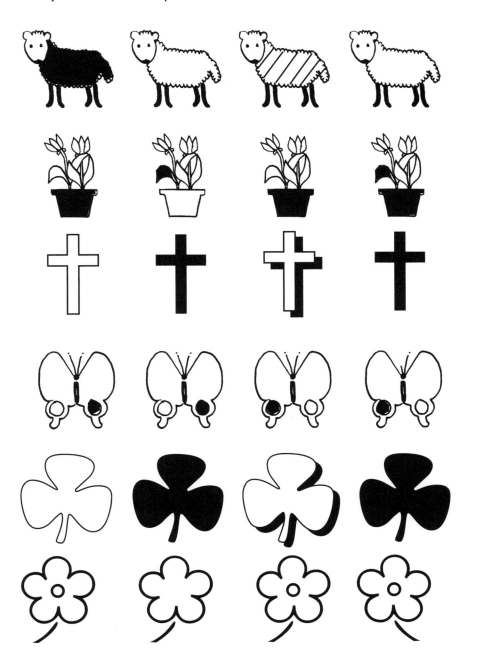

Long ago Christians drew pictures of Jesus that looked like this. Can you understand what they were trying to say about Jesus?

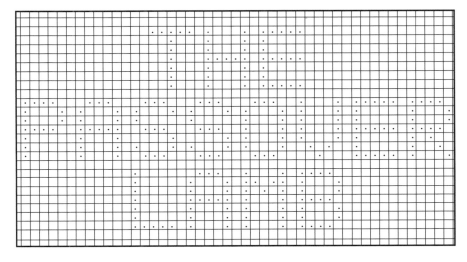

To find another name for Jesus, fill in the dotted squares.

A Father's Day Crossword Puzzle:
FAMOUS BIBLE FATHERS

Can you recognize these fathers?

Across

1. The father of Joseph and eleven other sons. (Genesis 35:24)
2. The father of Cain, Abel, and Seth. (Genesis 4:1, 2)
3. Jesus' earthly father. (Matthew 1:24, 25)
4. Jesus healed this father's sick little girl. (Luke 8:41, 42)
5. The father of the disciples James and John. (Matthew 4:21)

Down

6. The father of Ham, Shem, and Japheth. (Genesis 7:13)
7. The father of King David. (1 Samuel 16:1)
8. Our heavenly Father. (Philippians 2:11)
9. The father of Isaac. (Genesis 21:3)

CHILDREN'S BULLETIN

Do you remember who the Victorious Lamb is? How many of the symbols on the Lamb's flag can you recognize?

THX KZNGDVM VF GVD ZS NXQR

The message in this puzzle needs to be decoded. All ot the vowels have been replaced with other letters. Follow the code below to unscramble the message that Jesus' disciples were supposed to tell the people.

Replace all **Q**'s with **A**'s. Replace all **X**'s with **E**'s. Replace all **Z**'s with **I**'s. Replace all **V**'s with **O**'s.

Give thanks to the Lord for he is good . . . he gives food
to every creature. His love endures forever!
Psalm 136:1, 25

THANKSGIVING

How many jungle animals can you find? Color each of them.

We have many things to thank God for. Draw the food on the
table for these people who have bowed their heads to pray.

```
  1 □ □ □ | T |
  □ □ □ | H | □ □ □
      3 | A |
  4 □ □ □ | N | □ □ □
      □ □ | K | □ □ □
  6 □ □ □ | S |
```

Fill in the blanks with the correct words.

1. "Thanks be to God for his indescribable
   _____." (2 Corinthians 9:15)

2. "Thanks and . . . _____ be to our God."
   (Revelation 7:12).

3. "We always thank God . . . when we _____
   for you." (Colossians 1:3)

4. "I thank Christ Jesus . . . who has given me
   _____." (1 Timothy 1:12)

5. "For this reason I _____ before the Father."
   (Ephesians 3:14)

6. "Give thanks to him and _____ his name."
   (Psalm 100:4)

The fourth Thursday in November is proclaimed by the president of the United States to be a special day of Thanksgiving. This is a time for us to give special thanks to God. It is also a time when we remember the Pilgrims who came to America and who thanked God for their food, their new country, and their lives.

How many things can you find that don't fit in this picture of the first American Thanksgiving feast?

The first Thanksgiving feast was possible only because friendly Indians had taught the Pilgrims how to grow and cook American foods: corn, turkey, and cranberries.

Draw some of the people (farmers, grocery store clerks) who helped make YOUR feast possible.

CHILDREN'S BULLETIN

Give thanks to the Lord, for he is good. His love endures forever! Psalm 136:1

Today Is Food Shelf Sunday!

Draw you and your family here.

Fill this space with more food.

Give these people smiles as they get food.

Color the picture.

Check Ephesians 2:20 to discover who is on the bottom row.

IN·CHRIST·THE·WHOLE·BUILDING IS·JOINED·TOGETHER·AND RISES·TO·BECOME·A·HOLY TEMPLE·IN·THE·LORD

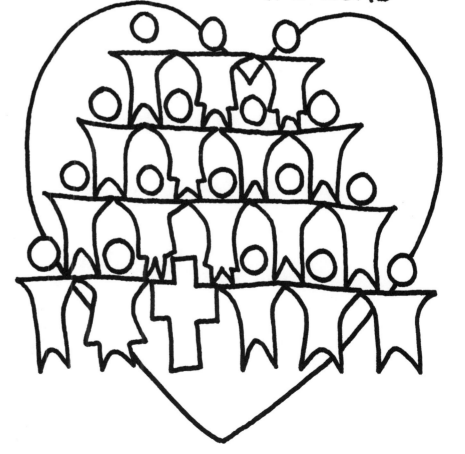

NEW YEAR 199__

CHILDREN'S BULLETIN

Do You Know?
What year will start next week? (fill in the number) _____
How many months are in a year? _____
How many days are in a year? _____
How old will our church be in this new year? _____

People like to plan for a new year; they make "resolutions"—plans to be better people. Have you made any New Year's resolutions? Try listing some here:

_____

_____

_____

_____

Each new year is very much like the last in spite of people's resolutions. But when God makes a new heaven and new earth, they'll be REALLY new and different!

January

starts a new year. One day God will start a new earth and heaven. For both God and us, this will be a time of . . .

Fill in all the dotted shapes to find the word.

Word Search

Find the underlined words in the box below.

Do not be <u>anxious</u> about anything, but in everything, by <u>prayer</u> and petition, with <u>thanksgiving</u>, present your <u>requests</u> to God. And the <u>peace</u> of God, which goes beyond all <u>understanding</u>, will guard your <u>hearts</u> and your <u>minds</u> in Christ <u>Jesus</u> .
Philippians 4:6–7

```
Q V X U R S T R A E H K Y
W G K S U S E J B U D E W
D P R A Y E R Y A X Y F S
O C S T S E U Q E R M F D
G K V D X X X G T N T H N
P E A C E S M X O H S V I
K E L Q X X B O T E M T M
Y G N I V I G S K N A H T
U N D E R S T A N D I N G
X L H K A N X I O U S O R
J J H F R J E J A S H V F
```

Hearts full of love for Jesus make us part of one family, however different we look!
Circle pictures of people with hearts for Jesus.

CHILDREN'S BULLETIN

Today is
All Nations
Heritage
Sunday.

We celebrate our different colors and faces.